ANDERS ZORN

REDISCOVERED

November 27–December 19, 1984

An exhibition organized by the Museum Studies Certificate Program
The University Art Museum, California State University, Long Beach

Edited by Jane K. Bledsoe

Cover:
Self Portrait with Model II, 1899
Etching
24.5 x 17.6 cm. (9⅝ x 7 in.)
Collection: Spencer Museum of Art, University of Kansas, Lawrence
    Gift of the Max Kade Foundation

The museum gratefully acknowledges the support and cooperation of the CSULB Foundation, Instructionally Related Activities Fund, Forty Niner Shops, and the School of Fine Arts and Department of Art. A portion of the museum's general operating funds for this fiscal year has been provided through a grant from the Institute of Museum Services, a Federal agency that offers general operating support to the nation's museums, and by a general operating support grant from the California Arts Council.

ACKNOWLEDGEMENTS

Anders Zorn Rediscovered has been made possible through the assistance of many individuals: Dr. Ingrid Aall, professor, Art Department, California State University, Long Beach; Brigitte Bergman, Lena Torslow Hansen, Raymond Lindgren and the members of the American Scandinavian Foundation of Los Angeles; Dr. Hans Henrik Brummer, director, Zornmuseet, Mora, Sweden; Bruce Davis, curator, Prints and Drawings, and Christine Vigiletti, assistant registrar, Los Angeles County Museum of Art; Lucinda Heyel Gedeon, acting curator, Grunwald Center for Graphic Arts, University of California, Los Angeles; Elna Johanson and the members of the Swedish American Historical Association of California; Gunnel Myhrberg, Swedish Information Service, New York; Ted Nittler, director, de ville galleries, inc., Los Angeles; and Ossian Quiding, former consul, Swedish Consulate, Los Angeles.

We wish to express our gratitude to Jane K. Bledsoe, Constance W. Glenn, Terry Chapman, Jamie G. Hoover and the other members of The University Art Museum staff. Their knowledge, support, and patience have been invaluable. We would also like to thank Craig Krull and Michelle Weigand for their efforts in the early stages of this project.

1984 Museum Studies Class
Wendell Eckholm
Anne B. Morris
Carrell Shaw
Karen Sirus
Mary R. Sullivan
Pamela C. Tippman

Anders and Emma Zorn in Stockholm, 1885
Photograph

INTRODUCTION

In searching for the focus of the 1984 museum studies exhibition the students became intrigued by the career of Anders Zorn and the phenomenon that it represents: namely, his international fame as a painter during his lifetime and his almost instant obscurity following his death in 1920. This exhibition, aptly called **Anders Zorn Rediscovered,** and its accompanying catalogue are testament to the diligent scholarship and perserverance of each member of the class. To Anne, Carrell, Karen, Mary, Pam, and Wendell I offer my congratulations and appreciation for a job well done.

This year also marks the tenth anniversary of the Museum Studies Certificate Program annual series of exhibitions. Founded in 1973 by Constance W. Glenn, the program is designed to train students for professional careers in the nation's 6,000-plus museums. An integral portion of this training is a two semester long class in which candidates for the certificate act as the staff of a museum and are responsible for the production, documentation, and presentation of an exhibition in The University Art Museum. From its inception, in which I was a fortunate participant as a member of the first class, until the present day the program has borne the unmistakable *empreinte* of Connie Glenn's vision, energy, and dedication to excellence. Although she is on sabbatical leave this semester, her dynamic leadership of the Museum Studies Program and The University Art Museum and her continuing role as teacher, mentor, and scholar has contributed significantly to the success of this exhibition.

Jane K. Bledsoe
Acting Director, The University Art Museum
Museum Studies Certificate Program

ANDERS ZORN
THE NEW CENTURY

About Anders Zorn someone has said: "He had God in his soul, and the Devil in his fingertips." Surely some supernatural power must have guided his hand, for since the time of Leonardo da Vinci there has never been a man of such versatile genius. It is enough that, with our own John [Singer] Sargent, he is one of the greatest portrait painters of recent times.[1]

Hiram Blauvelt, critic for the *American Magazine of Art*, wrote these words about Anders Zorn five years after his death in 1920, which ended an internationally acclaimed career that spanned more than forty years. Zorn was a very popular and well-known artist during his time, in favor with both the art critics and the European and American publics. Armand Dayot, a French art critic writing for *International Studio* in 1929, compared Zorn's work as an etcher with that of Rembrandt, stating that "since Rembrandt, no engraver has equalled Zorn in the interpretation of that abysmal mystery — the human figure."[2] Henri Focillon, renowned art historian, also said of Zorn, "He is a born master of graphic art, and one of the greatest ever. One can regard his etched work as an original force in the history of occidental thought during the nineteenth-century."[3] And, according to one critic, his work was so individual and so powerful that it was beyond comparison with that of other painters[4] and, instead, should be likened to the writings of Guy de Maupassant, a contemporary of Zorn's, who like Zorn was "impassionately in love with the sensual existence" and "capable of imparting to the spectator that almost startling sensation of the vehemence of life."[5] Indeed, Zorn's passion for life and art was so well noted by his contemporaries that his obituary in *The New York Times* postulated that:

[in the presence of such a life enhancing art,] it is safe to predict for Zorn a long fame. He anticipated the modern reaction from the languors and doubts that beset the world in the nineteenth-century, the effort to subdue irresolution and return to

Figure 1
En fiskare (Fisherman of St. Ives), 1887
Oil on canvas
128 x 86 cm. (50³/₈ x 33⁷/₈ in.)
Collection: National Collection of France

*the classic ideal of the sound mind in the sound body, the present impatience of
what is invalid and over-refined. His work is tonic.*[6]

      In light of Anders Zorn's widespread popularity and acclaim during his
lifetime, it is somewhat puzzling that interest in his work seems to have waned so quickly after
his death. His paintings and watercolors, with the exception of his commissioned portraits of
American socialites and public figures, have been collected by almost no major museums outside of Sweden, and mention of his works, or even name, is seldom made in any of the standard
art history survey texts. That an oversight of some magnitude has happened is certain; whether
or not it is deserved is another question, and one that may possibly be answered through a
survey of the major art movements that occurred during the time Zorn lived and worked.

      In the last quarter of the nineteenth-century, when Zorn was just beginning
to exhibit his work publicly, Paris was the center of attention for the international art community and the Impressionism of Renoir, Monet, and Degas was at the peak of its notoriety. Zorn
traveled to Paris in 1888, where, because of his extensive social contacts in the art world, he was
welcomed into influential art circles, met the major impressionist painters, and formed a lasting
friendship with the sculptor Rodin.[7] Although Zorn had experimented with an Impressionist
style in his painting *Fisherman of Saint Ives*, 1887 (figure 1), which was accepted for the Paris
Salon of 1888,[8] he seems to have been less influenced by the ideas of the Impressionist group
than he was by the painterly techniques of their brushwork and use of color, and continued to
work in his own individual direction.

The Impressionist influence had been felt in England as well during the 1870s and 1880s, with the American-born James McNeill Whistler, an acquaintance of Zorn's, as chief proponent. In the United States, too, during this time the style of Impressionism was being explored with Childe Hassam and J. Alden Weir leading the way. Amid much public furor, the Post-Impressionist works of Cézanne, Van Gogh, and Gauguin began to be shown in Paris in the late 1880s, and were soon followed by the energetic Fauvist paintings of Matisse and his followers. Finally the innovations of the Cubist painters Picasso, Braque, and Gris so thoroughly shook the international art community that our ideas about art were forever changed.

In Germany, the expressionism of the *Die Brücke* group began to emerge in 1905 and the compelling psychological portraiture of Ernst Ludwig Kirchner was seen for the first time. This movement was followed closely by the primitive and tribal-inspired works of the *Der Blaue Reiter* group led by Franz Marc and Wassily Kandinsky. Anders Zorn's portraiture, although technically precise and perhaps penetrating in clarity of vision, cannot be considered to be psychological in the sense of revealing inner states of being of the sitter or using color to interpret emotion. Zorn's work was confined much more to revealing only the surface of a subject's personality.

The early twentieth-century genre to which Zorn's work was most clearly related was that of the Ash Can School (1904–1913), but the American works were markedly more expressive in their use of color and in their depictions of everyday life. Zorn's *oeuvre* was much more subdued in content and in form, and seems rooted in a romanticism and attitude decidedly of the nineteenth-century. During the latter part of Zorn's career, Modernism became firmly established as the prevailing aesthetic and was expressed in a variety of forms ranging from the figurative abstractions of the Stieglitz group in the United States, to the mechanistic gestures of the Futurists in Italy, to the precision of Walter Gropius's Bauhaus group in Weimar, Germany, to the reductive Suprematism of the revolutionary Soviet artists.

As an internationally acclaimed artist and inveterate traveler, Anders Zorn certainly must have been aware of the changes that were happening in the art world at the turn of the century. In fact, the largest retrospective of his work to be presented during his lifetime took place at the Paris gallery of Durand-Ruel in 1906, at a time when Paris was reeling from the innovations of Matisse and the Fauves and was at the very threshold of the Cubist revolution. Yet Zorn chose to remain unaffected by Modernism, or at least by what it implied about artistic expression. Zorn was a realist painter at the time of the birth of abstraction; an illusionist when the avant-garde chose to deny the illusionistic tradition.

He was a champion of honesty, forthrightness, and simplicity — qualities which he admired in the American public and patrons who made him feel so much at home when there — and had a distrust of intellectualism,[10] which may have been rooted in his remembrances of his own modest origins. It was in the salons in both Europe and America that Zorn was most avidly accepted, salons which were both the symbolic and real targets of derision by the intellectually sophisticated new generation of artists. His permanent return to his Swedish hometown of Mora in 1896 may have been a retreat from a changing world in which his values were soon to be outmoded and of little but historical interest. Yet, he and his work were important to a particular time and generation; his choice to retain an allegiance to an era that in, retrospect, had so clearly ended may have been a statement more heroic than we think — or it may have been the self-serving gesture of an artist seeking to perpetuate the fame that was his. In either case, there is no disputing that Anders Zorn was an extremely talented artist and a perceptive chronicler of his time. It is the enigma of Zorn the man that remains with us.

Wendell Eckholm

FOOTNOTES

[1] Hiram Bellis Blauvelt, "Zorn's Finger Tips," *American Magazine of Art*, February 1925, p. 87.

[2] Armand Dayot, "The Brilliant Etchings of Anders Zorn," *International Studio*, July 1929, p. 32.

[3] Ibid., p. 36.

[4] For example, "How does he stand in relation to Monet and the Impressionists? Naturally, they have influenced his art, but to him Art did not involve merely a problem of optics and technique." (*The American Review of Reviews* [May 1910], p. 614.)

[5] Carl G. Lauren, "A Swedish Painter and Etcher: Anders Zorn," *International Studio*, Vol. 13, 1898, p. 166. See also: *The American Review of Reviews*, May 1910, p. 614.

[6] "Obituary," *The New York Times*, 29 August 1920.

[7] Elizabeth Broun, *Prints of Anders Zorn* (Lawrence, Kansas: The Spencer Museum of Art, University of Kansas, 1979), p. 10.

[8] Ibid.

[9] "With the modern artists he may be compared with Sargent, but, if his brush is more animated than that of the American master, it is decidedly less subtle. Mr. Sargent has a deeper insight into the character of his sitter. Zorn has been said to lack psychology in his portraits." (*American Art News* [October 16, 1920], p. 5.)

[10] Ingela Lind, "Looking Again at Anders Zorn," *Scandinavian Review*, Summer 1984, p. 23.

ANDERS ZORN
BIOGRAPHY

Anders Zorn was "born under a lucky star," according to his friend and fellow artist, Ernst Josephson. Indeed, it would seem that the life of this remarkable man was guided by an extraterrestrial force. From his early childhood on his grandfather's farm, Gruddgården, in central Sweden, Anders Zorn seemed destined to become an artist. Yet, his life was filled with paradoxical circumstances, powered by the opposing forces of adversity and fortune, of recurrent illness and boundless energy, of "exile" and acceptance, of wanderlust and a yearning for home. Home, as Zorn once said when asked where he was from, was nowhere; and yet, when he had tired of his worldwide wanderings, it was to the village of Mora in the rugged, central Swedish province of Dalecarlia that he returned.

Anders Zorn was born on February 18, 1860, to Grudda Anna Andersdotter and Leonard Zorn, a Bavarian brewery master of peasant ancestry. Zorn's father never married his mother, but he did commit to providing for his son's formal education when the boy was twelve.

Zorn's childhood in Mora was a happy one, although impoverished and typically Dalecarlian: "Early I learned to be useful: to help out the others at work as much as I could, watch over the sheep in the woods, carry home fir-twigs and chop them up to strew on the cowshed floor, help Grandpa at the anvil, sew, knit — in brief to lend a hand at just about anything."[1] In addition to helping his grandparents with the chores on the farm, he traveled with them to far off *säter*, or mountain pastures, shared the joy of seasonal feasts, and attended the Infant School at Mora. This relationship with his peasant grandparents and the agrarian values which they instilled in him were a powerful influence on his life.

It was evident when he was very young that Zorn had artistic talent and he could often be found sketching his surroundings, drawing portraits of friends, or carving small animals from wood scraps. ". . . then, in the evening, I would borrow Grandpa's knife to carve a two-legged horse in bark, for the bark wasn't strong enough to allow of [sic] four distinct legs. Sometimes I could borrow his carpenter's pencil to draw horses or figures on the back of a letter from my mother, which was all the paper we ever had."[2] Since artists had traditionally worked in the villages of Dalecarlia, art was perceived as a valid profession. Thus, Anders' budding talent was nurtured and encouraged from the beginning by family, friends, and teachers. At the Enköping Secondary School, which he attended from 1872–1875, the headmaster, instead of disciplining him for his lack of attention in class, allowed him to exchange music lessons for drawing lessons. He spent the summer holidays during these years with his mother near the Stockholm archipelago where she worked as a gardener for a brewer named Dölling. It was there that Anders learned that vast differences existed between the wealthy and the poor, that there were those who belonged and those who did not. Zorn's awareness of his being in the latter category would plague him wherever he went, save Mora, and was possibly the basis for the frequent bouts of depression and nervous exhaustion which would recur throughout his adult life.

Leonard Zorn died intestate, and although he had agreed to educate his son, the illegitimate Anders had no legal claim on his father's estate. However, with the help of the Swedish-Norwegian Consul General, he was granted three thousand Swedish crowns for his education by the Zorn family. In 1875, at the age of eighteen, with good school reports and a letter of recommendation introducing him to Anton Bolinder, an important Stockholm manufacturer, he enrolled in the Stockholm Academy of Art. In addition to his formal studies, Zorn attended night classes at the School of the Society for Applied Art and worked at a rented bench in a joiner's shop earning small but regular sums of money from his carvings. The income from his father's estate arrived irregularly, if at all, causing Zorn serious financial difficulty and constant worry. His personal charm, however, enabled him to win friendships and entry into the homes of the wealthy. It was this attribute, along with his talent, that would help him through a series of financial crises and promote his career as an artist, especially in the area of portraiture.

It was during this time that Zorn discovered watercolor at a memorial exhibition of paintings by Egron Lundgren. Intrigued by the "soft colors," he purchased a set of paints and began to work in this medium, painting *en plein air* during summers at Mora and in every spare moment at the academy. By 1879, Zorn, whose early portraits had been of corpses lying in state, had developed his skill as a portrait painter to the point where he could command a fee of fifty crowns. This was an important step toward financial independence, which until then had eluded him. During the winter of 1878–79, when the last of his inheritence was exhausted, he had been forced to accept a fifty crown a month allowance from the German colony in Stockholm. Zorn commented upon this period, "My inherent self-esteem went through a hard but useful school."[3]

11

Figure 2
I sorg (In Mourning), 1880
Watercolor
23 x 19.5 cm. (9 x 7¾ in.)
Collection: Nationalmuseum, Stockholm, Sweden

His artistic reputation was also advanced the following year when his water-color motif of a veiled woman, called *In Mourning*, 1880 (figure 2), received the acclaim of King Oscar and the art critic Carl Rupert Nyblom. The painting sold quickly and brought further commissions, along with an award of two hundred crowns from the academy. Zorn's relationship with the school had always been on shaky ground since he had been compelled to work for commissions, had neglected his studies, and had refused to accept the institution's conservative policies. In the spring of 1881 Zorn left school to begin his career as an artist.

He traveled first to England, where Egron Lundgren had painted, hoping to follow his example. With his friend Christian Bolinder he explored the lush greenness of the Thames Valley. London, however, was a disappointment and, after a brief visit to Paris, he traveled to Spain with Ernst Josephson. This would be the first of many visits to the land he had envisioned and he exclaimed on his arrival at Andalusia, "My dream has come true, and reality exceeds my dream."[4] Spanish scenes would become an important part of his early work. However, apparently exhausted from the rigors of travel and intense work, he suffered what was then described as a nervous breakdown.

His health restored, he returned to Paris where he was joined by Emma Lamm, the daughter of Stockholm merchant Martin Lamm, and her mother. He had first met this beautiful woman with captivating blue eyes while painting a portrait of her nephew. Ironically, Mrs. Lamm had unknowingly encouraged their romance when she commissioned Zorn to paint her daughter's portrait; later Emma and Anders became secretly engaged. During this period, Emma taught Zorn to enjoy museums and ". . . to take an interest in history, with art as object lessons."[5] It was also at this time that his Tangiers watercolor, *Cousins*, 1882, was well received by the 1882 Paris Salon, an honor which was welcome at a time when his work was being criticized in Sweden as too impressionistic.

Much to the surprise of his friends, Zorn chose to return to England rather than settle in Paris or Spain, both of which he had found stimulating. His instincts told him that London was the best place to make a name for himself as a watercolorist and, after a second summer in the Thames Valley with Bolinder, he stretched his financial resources to the limit in order to establish a fashionably located studio in Brook Street. Along with sales of his travel paintings, commissions from members of the Swedish-Norwegian Legation, from visiting Americans, and the English aristocracy kept Zorn afloat financially, but not without a struggle. It was during this stay in England, that he met the Swedish printmaker, Axel Haig, who became his friend and taught him the basics of etching, a technique that would become an increasingly important portion of Zorn's *oeuvre*. With the exception of short trips to Paris, Portugal, and Sweden, Zorn remained in London until 1885, when he returned to Stockholm to marry Emma Lamm.

During his 1882 visit to Paris, where he had first seen Japanese prints and the work of John Singer Sargent, Zorn began to dream of traveling to Japan and the United States. The avant-garde ideas emanating from Paris intrigued him but did not immediately penetrate his own work. Instead, it was the work of such masters as Rembrandt and Franz Hals that inspired him at that time. "As a rule," wrote Gerda Boëthius of that period, "Zorn seems to have been more influenced by older painters than by his contemporaries."[6]

After their wedding in the fall of 1885, Zorn and Emma began an extensive wedding trip which would take them to Germany, Vienna, Prague, Budapest, Constantinople (where he became gravely ill with typhus), Greece, Italy, Paris, London, and back to Sweden. Thus, Zorn had become a "true cosmopolitan," traveling from country to country seeking not only portrait commissions but also establishing friendships and valuable contacts around the world. The stimulation from this lifestyle seems to have been an essential element in Zorn's success as an artist.

In 1887, having fulfilled several portrait commissions in England and having painted *en plein air* during summers in Sweden, Zorn and his wife traveled once again, this time to North Africa and Spain. In rich, vigorously brushed watercolors he captured the luminosity of Algiers and Alhambra and returned to London with a portfolio full of salable paintings. Later that same year on their way back to Spain, the Zorns stopped at the artists' colony at St. Ives in southern England. It was here that Zorn first began to use oils. In this provocative environment, he worked feverishly, producing his first major oil painting, *The Fisherman of St. Ives*, 1887 (figure 1). This impressionistic work was sent with some hesitation to the 1888 Paris Salon, where, to Zorn's surprise, it received an honorable mention. The painting was subsequently bought by the French State for the Luxembourg Museum. Bolstered by this honor and the favorable criticism which followed, the Zorns decided to move to Paris, where they remained until 1896 in studios on Rue Daubigny and later on the Boulevard de Clichy. This new recognition, along with the influence of his friend and patron, London financier Ernest Cassel, brought Anders and Emma into the exclusive art circles of Paris where they became acquainted with such influential people as Antonin Proust, the directeur général des Beaux-Arts, and Armand Dayot, art critic and publisher of *Art et les Artistes*.

This time in Paris was a period of growth and change for Zorn. For the first time he felt that he belonged in the society of the influential and the wealthy. Painful boyhood memories began to fade and with increased self confidence he eagerly absorbed new, stimulating ideas from the Impressionists, from Japanese prints, and from Sargent and James McNeill Whistler, both of whom he had met in England. Zorn's success at the Paris Exposition and the Salon of 1888, as well as his growing reputation as a portraitist, brought him prosperity, allowing him more time for etching and impressionistic studies of indoor and outdoor light. He typically spent the summer months in Sweden painting robust peasant nudes bathing in the rare light of the long, northern summer nights.

Zorn seemed to revel in the cultural fermentation which boiled in Paris then and, when a split occurred among the French artists, could be found in the ranks of the new liberal exhibition society, the Champs de Mars Salon. Its first exhibition in 1890 proved to be a triumph for Zorn; his etchings, especially the portrait, *Rosita Mauri*, 1889 (see plate 11), which appeared in a full-page reproduction in the *Gazette des Beaux-Arts*, were acclaimed as miraculous, and thus, ". . . the doors were opened to the then very rich world of art."[7] Commissions for portraits and purchases of his work by wealthy Americans and Europeans enhanced Zorn's reputation as a young Swedish talent just as plans for the 1893 World's Columbian Exposition in Chicago were being made. An organizer of the event, Halsey C. Ives, sought Zorn's help in gathering together a representative collection of Swedish art. On their journey to the exposition Anders and Emma were received warmly into the homes of wealthy American art collectors and long-term friendships were formed with such prominent citizens as the Potter Palmers of Chicago, the Charles Deerings of Evanston, and Isabella Stewart Gardner of Boston. These and many other important Americans, including three presidents, would purchase works and commission portraits by Zorn. Frederick Keppel, a New York art dealer whom Zorn met on this first trip to the United States, kept the artist's work in the public eye for many years, arranging small, but highly publicized exhibits of recent portraits and etchings. Emma and Anders enjoyed the feeling of freedom in America and the open friendliness of its people so much that their first visit lasted for ten months and was followed by six more at varying intervals.

Zorn's international lifestyle continued for over a decade with regular visits to Paris, London, and the United States interspersed with more exotic trips to such places as Russia, Mexico, the Middle East, and Cuba. The rigors of his work schedule and the constant shuttling from place to place, while glamorous and stimulating, nevertheless, had eroded Zorn's physical and emotional health and he began to yearn for home. "It became impossible to divide the year among three essential places of work. Sweden meant too much to Zorn to allow him to reduce the time spent there."[8]

In the summer of 1888, while on one of his *plein air* excursions to Sweden, Zorn purchased a small piece of land in Mora adjacent to a church that his mother, widowed with small children, had inherited. He then moved a small cottage from his grandfather's farm to the site for her residence. The original intent of this move was to care for his mother, but owning this bit of homeland evidently fulfilled a personal need as well. Zorn wrote about his feelings at that time:

> *Never has there been a prouder landowner. From being poorer than anyone and heir to nothing, I was now the richest — Exile in foreign parts, the homeless had now a home for himself and his nearest.*[9]

When the decision was made in 1896 to change from an international lifestyle to one which was primarily Swedish (or Dalecarlian, to be more exact), Zorn enlarged the small cottage at Mora to become the present Zorn House and created a studio from a *seter* farmhouse dating back to the Middle Ages. He now had a home base to which he could return from his travels to paint and etch Swedish genre scenes and nudes. "Swedish subjects had always occupied a prominent place in Zorn's mind, and he has stated it was very refreshing to paint a bay in the Stockholm archipelago with nudes, or a genuine Mora milieu, whether out-of-doors or in the chiaroscuro inside the cottages."[10]

The move to Mora renewed the artist's interest in Swedish provincial culture and from this time until his death, he amassed an impressive collection of native architecture, paintings, sculpture, craftware, artifacts, and costumes that would later be housed at the Zornmuseet.[11] After the turn of the century the Zorns' life centered increasingly around their home in Mora, on its people, and on its culture. Emma and Anders founded an art school for young people and nurtured a revival of Dalecarlian festivals, folk dances and songs, crafts, and language. Many of Zorn's later works focused on these activities as during his last years "his life became identical with his work . . . ."[12]

This isolation did not diminish his reputation as an artist. More famous than ever, he was commissioned not only to do portraits of the aristocratic, the powerful, and the wealthy but also of kings, princes, and presidents, and, until the onset of World War I forced them to remain in Sweden, the Zorns maintained contacts in England, France,

Germany, Italy, and America. The culmination of this period for Zorn was a 1906 Paris retrospective, when the Durand-Ruel Gallery was filled with his oils, etchings, watercolors, and sculpture. Zorn felt that this was the greatest honor that had ever been bestowed upon him; it was a triumph for the artist and for the art of his nation.

For solitude and undisturbed painting, Zorn created an idyllic hideaway at the foot of Mount Gopsmor in an isolated wilderness area by Lake Siljan. Here he would paint for weeks at a time, joined occasionally by those to whom he had extended a standing invitation: the young people of neighboring villages and his closest friends. Equally precious to the artist was the time spent on his yacht, the *Mejt*, in the Stockholm archipelago. As it must have been for his Viking ancestors, the adventure and the challenge of exploring the sea, powered by the wind, was alluring, even to the end of his life when his health was failing. He died August 22, 1920, a few months after his mother's death.

The illegitimate son of a bottle washer and a brewery master, perhaps born under a lucky star as his friend had imagined, was honed by circumstances to a steely spiritual hardness which not only sustained him through poverty, "exile," and ill health, but propelled him towards the achievement of his goal: to be a great artist, following in the footsteps of the masters he admired. When his life had ended, his work could be found in many of the world's museums and private collections, he had been welcomed as a friend into the mansions and palaces of the wealthy and the noble, and most importantly, he had found his true home in the copses, lakes, and mountains of Dalecarlia.

> *Zorn, . . . whose name is known to the whole world, was partly a cosmopolitan, partly a primitive Swede, or more correctly, a Dalecarlian.*[13]

Anne B. Morris

FOOTNOTES

[1]Dan Hofstader, "Painter-Prince: the return of Anders Zorn," *The New Criterion*, January 1984, p.27.

[2]Ibid.

[3]Gerda Boëthius, *Zorn, Swedish Painter and World Traveler*, (Stockholm: Rabin and Sjogren, 1959), p.23.

[4]Ibid., p.36.

[5]Ibid., p.42.

[6]Ibid., p.36.

[7]Ibid., p.89.

[8]Ibid., p.107.

[9]Ibid., p.77–79.

[10]Ibid., p.113.

[11]Emma continued to live in Mora until her death in 1942; she established the museum in 1939, having shared her husband's love for the people of Dalecarlia and its culture.

[12]Karl Asplund, *Anders Zorn, His Life and His Work*, ed. Geoffry Holme, trans. Henry Alexander (London: The Studio, Ltd., 1921), p.9.

[13]Ibid., p.1.

ANDERS ZORN
AMERICAN PATRONAGE

Anders Zorn was initially introduced to the American public in 1893 when he was appointed Swedish Commissioner to the World's Columbian Exposition. This trip was the first of seven that the artist would make to America as his fondness for the country grew. He found its potential endless and the openness and sincerity of the people led him to comment that, "Their frank, straightforward manner suits my nature. I've never really been able to stand European city folks' ceremonious ways and artificial customs . . . over there when they say, 'He is all right,' all doors open to the foreigner, which Europeans cannot understand."[1]

Zorn's American commissions were dependent upon the contacts he made. Through his presence and the exhibition of his work at the World's Columbian Exposition, he became much sought after by eminent social, political, and business leaders. Berthe Honoré Palmer, or Mrs. Potter Palmer, as she was more widely known, was the leader of Chicago society and chairman of the Board of Lady Managers of the exposition. While in Paris in 1891, Mrs. Palmer had bought a brewery scene by Zorn and made arrangements to have him paint a full length portrait of her which was to be exhibited in the Arts Palace of the Exposition (figure 3). Though there had been some dissension over giving a man (rather than a woman) the commission, Mrs. Palmer stuck by her decision. The fact that Zorn's style was impressionistic with ". . . elements of fantasy and idealization . . ."[2] may have attracted her. In Zorn's portrait, ". . . Mrs. Palmer appeared as a vision. The gavel in her hand glowed like a fairy wand."[3] Comments by the contemporary press were not favorable and suggested the painting was unfinished and technically careless. Chicago newspapers excused these shortcomings by reporting that Zorn had injured his wrist in a riding accident (in actuality he had broken his collar bone) and had to finish the portrait with his left hand. Gossip had it that Mrs. Palmer had ordered Zorn away when he allegedly made improper advances, causing the portrait to remain unfinished. Despite the critical response to the painting, Mrs. Palmer was quite pleased and commented on its

Figure 3
Mrs. Potter Palmer, 1893
Oil on canvas
257.5 x 141.6 cm. (101⅜ x 55¾ in.)
Collection: The Art Institute of Chicago, Potter Palmer Collection

"brilliant artistic qualities," though saying that she could not judge the degree of the likeness.[4] The portrait was shown in the Paris Salon the next year and was very well received.

Isabella Stewart Gardner was another influential woman with whom Zorn made contact at the World's Columbian Exposition. She was a leader of Boston society, a position acquired through her strong personality and her marriage to John Lowell (Jack) Gardner, a prominent Bostonian businessman. Mrs. Gardner had a great interest in art and the money to collect it. Her fascination with Zorn and his work made his entrance into Boston society extremely smooth. Mrs. Gardner came to Chicago for the exposition and was favorably impressed by Zorn's oil painting, *Interior of an Omnibus in Paris*. According to contemporary accounts a man was standing nearby and when she questioned him as to whether the work was for sale, he replied that it was. She then inquired what he knew of the artist, Zorn. When he responded that he was Zorn, she exclaimed, "Yourself, indeed! Well, I feel sure we shall soon be enemies . . . or else very, very fast friends. You shall come today for tea."[5] She purchased the painting for $1,600 and from that time on Isabella Gardner became not only a close friend and patron of Zorn's, but also an avid promoter of his work. She persuaded friends to have their portraits painted and even convinced the Museum of Fine Arts in Boston to give him an exhibition.[6]

Zorn's first portrait of Isabella Stewart Gardner was an etching. Although she purportedly did not care for the piece, she nevertheless gave several copies to collectors of the artist's work, including the industrialist Charles Deering. Three years later Mrs. Gardner was again portrayed by Zorn. This work, in oil, was painted in Venice where the Zorns were the Gardners' guests at the Palazzo Barbaro (see plate 2). The story is told that one evening during a Venetian festival Mrs. Gardner had gone out onto the balcony to view the fireworks display. Suddenly she burst into the drawing room to summon the others. Her vibrant entrance so stunned Zorn that he decided to paint her as she appeared at that moment.

> *Mrs. Jack (Gardner), her hands pressing apart the glass doors, seemed to come forward joyously. Her pale yellow dress echoed a distant golden flare against the night sky. The famous pearls hung far below her waist and at the end of them a ruby glowed, while in the sky behind, the color was repeated in the red streak of a rocket. Zorn did not flatter Mrs. Jack overmuch — she was neither pretty, nor too young — but a woman full of vitality, in love with Venice and in love with life.*[7]

Although the portrait was not well received by contemporary critics, one of whom called the painting ". . . a mere sketch, an impression . . ."[8] it is now thought to be the best Zorn ever painted.[9] Zorn himself once remarked about its beauty, "Alas, all my subjects are not Mrs. Gardner and the background not the Canale Grande."[10] Mr. Gardner had no recorded comment on the work except for an entry in his journal, "Oct. 22 . . . Zorn finished picture of Mrs. G. in window."[11]

While both Mrs. Palmer and Mrs. Gardner promoted Zorn among their many friends, others learned of him through the exposition, the press, and various galleries that exhibited his work. Zorn's patrons bought not only his portraits, but his oils, watercolors, and etchings of nudes and genre scenes. His prominent clients included the Vanderbilts (who bought the painting *The Waltz*); the industrialist, Andrew Carnegie; New York banker and art collector, Henry Marquand; the vice president of Northern Pacific Railroad, Colonel Daniel Lamont; and philanthropist and member of the Busch Brewing family, Adolphus Busch. While the majority of Zorn's patrons were in the East and Midwest, his popularity was so widespread that several were as distant as California.

One of the patrons with whom Zorn became especially intimate was Charles Deering. The artist often stayed at the Deering home in Evanston, Illinois, where on successive visits he painted portraits of many members of the family. At the time, the Deerings had the most extensive collection of his etchings, as well as several of his genre scenes and nudes. It was on Deering's estate in the summer of 1893 that Zorn fell from a horse and broke his collar bone. This occurrence led to the aforementioned completion of Mrs. Palmer's portrait with his left hand. Because he had many pending commissions, he also painted a portrait of Charles Deering's daughter in the same manner.

Several of Zorn's commissioned works were portraits of men in public office — Presidents William Howard Taft and Grover Cleveland commissioned paintings and etchings, and President Theodore Roosevelt, Vice President James Sherman and Senator Nelson Aldrich had portraits painted. In 1911, while Taft was posing for Zorn, the President's preoccupation with former President Theodore Roosevelt's planned challenge for the Republican nomination caused the artist much concern. " 'The President is so weary that it shows in his face,' Zorn told Taft's secretary of Commerce and Labor, Charles Nagel, 'Can't you come over and talk to him so I can paint him as he really is?' Nagel tried, but Taft remained unchanged."[12] As a result, Zorn's portrait of Taft is noted for its honesty and expressiveness and stands as evidence of Zorn's ability to capture the mood of a sitter in a few fluid brushstrokes.

As was the case with so many of Zorn's patrons, he became a personal friend of President and Mrs. Cleveland. He was especially affected by the young Mrs. Cleveland and, having just completed her portrait, he remarked, "God, how stately and beautiful, and those arms, that neck, that bust worthy to be kissed by a thousand lips and now scarcely to be revealed to mortals."[13] Zorn and President Cleveland developed such a rapport that it is said that they once shared a bottle of bourbon on the edge of the White House bathtub. Not all of Zorn's commissions, however, went as smoothly as the Clevelands'. Henry Clay Pierce, the Saint Louis petroleum engineer, appears to have been Zorn's most problematic patron. Zorn painted Pierce's portrait (figure 4) and that of his wife and daughter in 1899. When the finished works were presented, Pierce was not satisfied with any of the three and demanded that many

Figure 4
Henry Clay Pierce, 1899
Oil on canvas
152 x 107 cm. (59¾ x 42⅛ in.)
Collection: Nationalmuseum, Stockholm, Sweden

changes be made before he would make payment. Zorn made several alterations, including the reduction of the size of Pierce's legs, but when the works were submitted again for Pierce's approval, he was still displeased and would not accept or pay for them. A widely publicized lawsuit followed, with Zorn suing for $12,000. After some time the case was settled in Zorn's favor and Pierce was made to pay Zorn $13,000 (the original claim, plus interest). Even though public sympathy was with Zorn, the extensive publicity upset him a great deal. Pierce, who claimed throughout the ordeal that he would burn his portrait, did not keep that vow — the painting was sold to the Ehrich Gallery in New York in 1934 for a mere $275.[14]

During Zorn's lifetime he enjoyed great critical acclaim and public acceptance in America. He was touted as the "Painter Prince"[15] and his etchings were compared to Rembrandt's. His works were featured in renowned New York galleries such as Frederick Keppel & Co. and M. Knoedler & Co., Inc. and were hung in private collections among works by Rembrandt, Tintoretto, El Greco, Velasquez, Monet, and Degas. Among his friends were Samuel Clemens, Stanford White, Daniel Frederic MacMonnies, and John Singer Sargent.

Zorn's painting style was compared to that of Sargent, Giovanni Boldini, the Italian portraitist, and Joaquin Sorolla, the noted Spanish Impressionist.[16] Although Zorn rivalled the other portraitists of the time in the number of commissions he received, portraits always remained a means of financial support rather than his true "aesthetic affection,"[17] which was always for the robust Swedish female nude.

In spite of the advent of Modernism, the popularity of Zorn's paintings remained intact. As a dynamic, personable man, Zorn created a flamboyant public image —

22

socializing with the wealthy and famous as well as painting their portraits — and it was not until his death in 1920 that sales began to decline. While there was a lapse in the popularity of the work of many of the society painters and more conservative artists in the early years of the century, many have regained status with the recent re-examination of American Impressionist painting as a whole. However, the resurgence of scholarly interest in Zorn's work — his nudes, genre scenes, and portraiture — has only recently begun. Elizabeth Broun focused on his etchings in the 1979 exhibition *The Prints of Anders Zorn* for the Spencer Museum of Art at the University of Kansas, while the Swedish Nationalmuseum in Stockholm is in the planning stages of a retrospective exhibition to be presented in 1986 — an exhibition which may well bring the critical evaluations of Anders Zorn's work to full cycle.

Carrell Shaw

FOOTNOTES

[1] Dan Hofstadter, "Painter Prince: the return of Anders Zorn," *The New Criterion*, January 1984, p. 27.

[2] Jeanne Madeline Weimann, *The Fair Women* (Chicago: Academy of Chicago, 1981), p. 580.

[3] Ibid.

[4] Ibid.

[5] Hofstadter, p. 27.

[6] *Anders L. Zorn* opened March 7, 1894, at the Museum of Fine Arts, Boston.

[7] Louise Tharp, *Mrs. Jack* (Boston: Little, Brown and Company, 1965), p. 181.

[8] Ibid.

[9] Aline Bernstein Saarinen, *The Proud Possessors* (London: Weidenfeld and Nicholson, 1958), p. 25.

[10] Ibid.

[11] Tharp, p. 181.

[12] Hofstadter, p. 31.

[13] "Recalling a Quarrel: Portrait of Henry Clay Pierce, by Anders Zorn," *Art Digest*, January 1, 1934, p. 17.

[14] Hofstadter, p. 31.

[15] Ibid., p. 26.

[16] Ibid., p. 27.

[17] Ibid., p. 30.

Plate 1
Untitled (Scandinavian Maid?), 1889
Oil on board
35.6 x 35.6 (14 x 14 in.)
Courtesy of de ville galleries, inc., Los Angeles

25

Plate 2
Isabella Stewart Gardner, 1895
Oil on canvas
91 x 66 cm. (35³/₄ x 26 in.)
Collection: Isabella Stewart Gardner Museum, Boston, Massachusetts
Not in exhibition

Plate 3
William Taussig, 1897
Oil on canvas
81.3 x 66 cm. (32 x 26 in.)
Collection: The J.B. Speed Art Museum, Louisville, Kentucky

27

Plate 4
Frances Folsom Cleveland (Mrs. Grover), 1899
Oil on canvas
137.1 x 92 cm. (54 x 36¼ in.)
Collection: National Portrait Gallery, Smithsonian Institution, Washington, D.C.
Gift of Mrs. Frances Payne

28

Plate 5
Badande kullor i bastun (Dalecarlian Girls Having a Bath), 1906
Oil on canvas
86 x 53 cm. (33⅞ x 20⅞ in.)
Collection: Nationalmuseum, Stockholm, Sweden
Not in exhibition

29

Plate 6
Mrs. Dan Cameron, 1900
Oil on canvas
147.3 x 113.3 cm. (60 x 44½ in.)
Collection: National Museum of American Art, Smithsonian Institution, Washington, D.C.
Gift of Anonymous Donor

Plate 7
Flickan från Elfdalen (The Girl from Elfdalen), n.d.
Oil on canvas
90.1 x 60.9 cm. (35½ x 24 in.)
Collection: The Minneapolis Institute of Arts, Lillian Z. Turnblad Fund

Plate 8
Mrs. Charles Deering, n.d.
Monotype
31.5 x 23.5 cm. (12³/₈ x 9¹/₄ in.)
Collection: The Art Institute of Chicago

32

ANDERS ZORN
STYLE

In the depth of his heart he would rather conquer the subject, retain it, explain it, and communicate to others in his own way the pleasure his eyes had experienced . . . He once explained to me the joy he felt in revealing the beauty of a subject through his brush, in making the spectator stop and look at Nature in a new way, a Nature more rich and beautiful — more Zornesque.[1]

Art comes into being as a result of man's visual confrontation with the world, a response to the physical, formal aspects of a subject, analyzed and translated into a creation. Anders Zorn's creations in painting and etching document the impressions of a world traveler via his visual confrontations with many cultures. "An artist who was past master in finding the essential in everything, who in an almost supernatural way, could conjure up on canvas an object so rich in life sap, so full blooded, that reality seemed tame beside it, was Anders Leonard Zorn."[2]

Zorn grew up in an environment full of chiaroscuresque landscapes, and vivid impressions of farm life. The glistening lakes, light summer evenings, white nights, and twilight typical of Sweden formed his artistic vision and acted as the tutor of his developing aesthetic perceptions. He lived in a one room farmhouse where daylight filtered through windows, and comingled with firelight to create form, value, and texture, and illuminated the shadowy recesses of the Mora cottage. The visions of Mora continually delighted Zorn and provided "generative and restorative influences"[3] in his later life when he returned home between his travels.

In addition to his childhood in Mora, Zorn gathered inspiration from his numerous travels to England, France, Spain, Germany, and the United States. The peripatetic artist also visited Russia, Cuba, Mexico, Palestine, Algeria, Egypt, Constantinople, and the North Pole. The appeal of his creative endeavors and the force of his personality in one country was the ticket, in acclaim and earnings, for travel to another. He also seemed to use the momentum of his travels to foster his creativity and has been described as a continual searcher for new sensations to stimulate subject matter for his paintings.[4]

Zorn's formal training, from 1875 to 1881, was at the Royal Academy of Fine Arts in Stockholm, combined with woodworking techniques learned through the School of the Society for Applied Art. His earliest drawings were noted for a remarkable individuality, clarity, firmness, and for suggesting movement by capturing the rhythm of his subjects.[5] In the academy years, Zorn's two most successful drawings, *The Artist's Mother*, 1877, and *Grandmother*, 1877, demonstrated his talent for analyzing the character of his models, portraying their features and capturing the essence of their personalities; they are renowned for the love and compassion which radiates from them. Discussions at the academy focused on *valeur*[6] painting and its connection to *plein air* painting, color theories, the importance of blue, the pros and cons of underpainting, the use of toned or white ground, and considerations of whether or not black was a color. Heavy restrictions with regard to composition and color, combined with interminable discussion of theory, with almost no latitude for the expression of emotion, were depressing to most of the young artists of the 1870s. Despite the restrictions, Zorn remained at the academy six years in order to learn basic skills.

Zorn's first ambition was to become a sculptor and it is apparent that a sensitivity to sculptural form remained an important aspect of his work throughout his life. After seeing the work of Egron Lundgren (1815–1875), Stockholm born watercolorist, he decided to become a painter.[7] Zorn's admiration for Lundgren's style, reflected in the use of responsive line, delicate color, and contemporary motifs, finally led him to England to glean Lundgren's cultural inspirations.

Disappointed with England, he traveled to Paris, then to Spain with a colleague, Ernst Josephson. Josephson was the leader of a group of Swedish radical reformers who had fled to Paris because they believed the Stockholm Academy's conservative teachings stifling to the spirit of artistic development. Josephson was influenced by the development of sculpture and painting in France, the close study of nature, and the Impressionist revolution. Zorn's association with Josephson proved beneficial, introducing Zorn to the artistic and political philosophies of the Swedish radicals. Although he gained artistic support from Josephson, they parted in Cadiz and Zorn stayed on to paint Spanish beauties and associate with the Swedish artists August Hagborg, Axel Haig, Carl Gustaf Hellqvist, Hugo Salmson, and Norwegian artists Fritz Thaulow, Frithiof Smith-Hald, and Eilif Petersen. Zorn organized an exhibit of Swedish art in Madrid which received favorable attention from the critics. During this period, Zorn was also exposed to the work of Velazquez, Goya, and Raeburn, which proved instrumental in the further development of his style.

Zorn's Spanish watercolors proved to be very popular because of their impressionistic character. Their light color key, casual color fusions, and distinct tonal values in the figural masses radiate over the surfaces, illustrating successful *valeur* qualities. Zorn depicted intense light by using warm yellows and put emphasis on movement and atmosphere through color contrasts and composition. The Iberian atmosphere and the Spanish beauties and Gypsies, with their pale faces and dark melancholy eyes, offered variety to his themes (see plate 9). With regard to the Gypsy models he wrote: "I painted with a stimulus and a pleasure that I had never experienced before. I was both spiritually and physically in my element."[8] According to critics at the time, "happiness" emanated from these works. They also claimed Zorn had become the artistic heir to Lundgren in style and sentiment and that he had surpassed his mentor in 1880 with a painting called *In Mourning* (figure 2).[9] He now had gained a better understanding of the plasticity of the facial structure and his colors contained a depth which had not been attained by Lundgren.[10]

At the urging of Julius Kronberg, a Swedish colleague who raved of the richness of Italian subject matter, Zorn decided to go to Rome. There he exchanged artistic philosophies with Carl Skånberg who had associated with the Impressionist painters in Normandy and as a result, was able to answer "Zorn's questions regarding the principles of *plein air* painting and Impressionism."[11] Skånberg's landscapes had a fresh, airy, clear, and exquisite quality. It is believed Zorn learned to use pearl grey tones from Skånberg's *Santa Maria della Salute in the Rain.*

In 1882, Zorn returned to England, became involved in the expatriate Swedish art colony there, and learned etching from Axel Haig. Watercolors had given Zorn a variety of skills which were readily transferable to this medium. Zorn's early etchings exhibit a "detailed finesse, earnest realism and a vernal and stimulating touch of the artist's joy of discovery."[12] His continual interest in interior lighting problems led to compositions in which light appeared from darkness with back lighting on faces to achieve a chiaroscuro effect. Parallel line masses, which became the mark in his plates, produced value variations and enhanced atmospheric conditions. An example of this technique is seen in his first eching, a self-portrait created in 1889, which was considered to be in the impressionist style. The most renowned work illustrating this approach is *Rosita Mauri*, 1889 (see plate 11). An 1892 portrait of Ernest Renan, the idealist philosopher, artist, poet, and scholar, so accurately reflected his character that some considered it comparable to the work of Rembrandt and one of the greatest etched portraits of all time. Only a few essential lines accentuate the form and countenance, capturing the subject's attitude and personality with light and linear treatment. These same qualities are evident in the portrait, *Jean Baptiste Faure*, the famous French baritone. An affinity with Rembrandt was also said to exist in the pathos of old age depicted in the 1911 works *Mona* and *Djos Mats*. Dr. Karl Asplund, in *Anders Zorn: His Life and Work*, states that these two works are

35

"Rembrandtesque in the way in which the artist has made the light play over the furrowed faces."[13] From 1911, the motifs for his etchings centered around genre scenes, instead of the previous focus on portraiture and nudes. He made seven to eleven etchings per year for the rest of his life, becoming so eminent that his work overshadowed that of all other Swedish graphic artists of the period. The etching process served as not only a way to make deep and difficult studies but also as a relaxing break from the intensity and exhaustion he experienced while painting portraits.

Zorn's serious works in oil began in the late 1880s. He became known internationally for his restricted palette of four colors; white, vermillion, ochre, and ivory black[14] and for pushing it to achieve coloristic effects as if playing "on a sensitive instrument."[15] By using greys and browns he developed atmospheric tones with somber color keys yet maintained a richness of color in order to achieve a close portrayal of reality. In December of 1882, he attended an exhibition in Paris which changed his creative perceptions and simplified his style. He was enchanted by the Japanese art in the exhibit and impressed by Sargent's *The Spanish Dance* for its motif and treatment.[16] Works by Lepage, Manet, and Degas offered new interpretations of perspective and approaches to mass. A use of diagonal composition derived from the Japanese had replaced the classically balanced compositions. The oriental feeling for line, texture, and color was united with the modern European taste for the observation of nature. The influences of French Impressionism became apparent in a delicate work entitled *Le Tub*, where his use of subtle tones of grey and rose introduced new qualities to his work. As his own characteristic style continued to form, a lengthy sweeping brushwork evolved and he became more of a colorist, employing warmer tones of brown, grey, yellow and gold. He often used strong patches of pigment to depict the effects of light and shading in interior and exterior studies.

Zorn's painting with oils displayed well integrated compositions involving strong tones, a pictorial grace and a high horizontal focus. Oils allowed him to attain more expressive effects than watercolor because they provided greater resources for plasticity, color richness, and atmosphere. Zorn's later oils also displayed a stronger impression of space by means of oblique perspective; one work in which this appears is *The Fisherman of St. Ives*, 1888 (figure 1). With its delicate tonal qualities, the painting was a success at the Paris salon in 1888 and as a result, critics compared Zorn's art to Paul Albert Besnard's.

Four of Zorn's portraits from the year 1889, continually mentioned and reproduced for their impressionistic qualities, are *Coquelin, Mme. Rikoff, Portrait of the Artist* (commissioned by the Uffizi Gallery), and *Charles Armitage. Coquelin* has often been mentioned as a major contribution to the art world of the period. These works also exhibit the

Figure 5
Mormor (Grandmother), 1889
Birchwood
16 cm. (6¼ in.)
Courtesy of Zornmuseet, Mora, Sweden

characteristics which formed the basis for Zorn's mature style: long sweeping brushwork, economic use of vivid colors, a somber harmony, strong lighting, and informal Impressionism.

After Zorn's first visit to the United States in 1893, his paintings became more plastic but less pictorial and he began employing a more pronounced color palette. His portraits of Americans expressed the appreciation and admiration he had for them, each one depicting a strong individuality in its straight-forward austere realism. Gerda Boëthius makes reference to Zorn's style:

> *Zorn and Sargent are often compared and indeed there are many similarities between them but at the same time there are many distinct differences . . . Unlike Sargent and Besnard he used no tricks to render convincingly the relationship between a figure or a volume and its environment. He developed the impressionistic technique in a unique and refined manner, often defining an outline by another value. He succeeded in finding the coloristic qualities even in the men's prosaic clothing.[17]*

It was observed and noted that his art displayed a tension between color, surface, and plasticity. In keeping with his early interest in sculpture, he also created works in wood, bronze, and clay. His favorite media was wood, especially birchwood. He enjoyed working with it in his leisure time, carving statuettes of women (*Gryvel*, 1905) or small female figures as the handles of spoons and knives. A bust entitled *Mormor*, 1889 (figure 5), was dismissed as a careless rendition, although some said it had "a refinement a la Rodin."[18] When working in clay, plaster, or bronze instead of wood, he was considered a naturalist. The work *Faun and Nymph*, 1895, typified his naturalist style through the employment of an unpolished surface and antique

Figure 6
Zorn Working on the Gustav Vasa Statue, 1902
Photograph
Courtesy of Zornmuseet, Mora, Sweden

patina. In reference to Zorn's work, Rodin stated at an banquet "that there were only two great sculptors — himself and Zorn!"[19]

The realization of the *Gustav Vasa* monument, a work consuming most of Zorn's time during 1901 and 1902 (figure 6), was believed to have influenced his painting style and expanded his awareness of culture and history. Gustav Erikson Vasa, a hero in Mora in 1520, helped to organize peasants to drive the oppressive Danes out of their territory. He succeeded and became the founder and first King of Sweden. The site chosen for the sculpture was the exact spot where Vasa had once made a revolutionary speech to the peasants of Mora. The statue was Zorn's gift to the village as a symbol of his nationalism. The figure's realistic, simple and dignified appearance creates a spiritual expression exuding monumentality.[20] The unveiling was on July 11, 1902, and he wrote in his notes, "This was really one of the greatest days in my life. Being a painter I felt most deeply my triumph as a sculptor."[21] At a later time, a letter to his wife included this statement: "Yes, I certainly feel that the 11th July was the culmination of my life."[22]

One of his best known sculptures is entitled *The Morning Bath*, 1908. The original is in the artist's garden at Mora, and a reproduction was commissioned by Herman Friedlander, presented to Stockholm, and erected in front of the Royal Academy of Arts. It is a classical figure of a Dalecarlian girl squeezing a sponge, a figure which seems to have stepped out of one of his oil paintings.[24] Zorn felt that these figures were very successful in the realistic modelling of the female form and he experienced intense pride and gratification in creating them.

Zorn alternated between several media to cultivate skills that were transferable to another medium, to solve artistic problems, to achieve financial security, or to alleviate boredom, and in doing so, developed a powerful *oeuvre*. However, inherent in his employment of each media are similarities in subject matter, content, and technique. His subjects ranged from genre settings and exotic, picturesque, or nude figures to the famous personages of each country in which he traveled. Of the three, he preferred to portray the nude female form. He did his most expressive works when he had an emotional involvement with the subject, consequently he painted relatives and close friends with profundity and passion.

The Swedish countryside and the Stockholm archipelago provided other themes and variations with foliage and the effects of water in ever-changing atmospheric conditions. Interior and exterior scenery, countryside folk activities, and village inhabitants enjoying daily routines were repeated motifs, especially in the later years. He depicted people working in breweries, harvesting, fishing, dancing, going to church, and baking bread, demonstrating that he was able to "find interesting material for his brush in almost anything."[24]

Zorn's works are characterized by sensual colors, shapes and textures, unity, balance, and spatial treatment — all uniting to create a unique configuration of visual qualities. His compositions tell stories which emphasize sentimentality and communicate life from the perspective of his personal knowledge and experience.

Pamela C. Tippman

FOOTNOTES

[1]Karl Asplund, *Anders Zorn, His Life and Work*, ed. Geoffrey Holm, trans. Henry Alexander. (Chicago: Kroch Company, 1921), p. 85.

[2]Emil Hanover, Carl Lauren, and Jens Thiis, *Scandanavian Art* (London: Humphrey Milford Oxford University Press, 1922), p. 188.

[3]Gerda Boëthius, *Zorn, An International Swedish Artist, His Life and Work* (Stockholm: Nordish Rotogravyr, 1954), p. 9.

[4]Asplund, p. 19.

[5]Boëthius, p. 10.

[6]*Valeur* is a technique by which several colors are run together, yet controlled to produce subtle tonal variations in such a manner that the viewer has the illusion of seeing and creating his own imaginative forms. (Gerda Boëthius, *Zorn, Swedish Painter and World Traveller* [Stockholm: Raber and Sjogren. 1959], p. 24.)

[7]Boëthius, *Zorn, Swedish Painter and World Traveller*, p. 21.

[8]Boëthius, *Zorn, International Swedish Artist*, p. 17.

[9]See essay, ANDERS ZORN: BIOGRAPHY, this catalog.

[10]Asplund, p. 13.

[11]Boëthius, *Zorn, Swedish Painter and World Traveller*, pp. 40, 42.

[12]Asplund, p. 61.

[13]Ibid., p. 70.

[14]Ivory black is a pigment obtained from calcined ivory or bones and was considered of great value to the painter. (Jules Adeline, *The Adeline Art Dictionary* [New York: Frederick Ungar Publishing Co., 1966], p. 215.)

[15]Boëthius, *Zorn, Swedish Painter and World Traveller*, p. 105.

[16]Ibid., pp. 40, 42.

[17]Boëthius, *Zorn, International Swedish Artist*, p. 56.

[18]Asplund, p. 77.

[19]Ibid., p. 78.

[20]Boëthius, *Zorn, International Swedish Artist*, p. 58.

[21]Ibid., p. 60.

[22]Ibid.

[23]Asplund, p. 78.

[24]Hanover, Laurin, Thiis, p. 191.

ANDERS ZORN
NUDES

Of the three main areas of subject matter upon which Anders Zorn concentrated — commissioned portraits, genre scenes, and nudes — the latter was perhaps the most fascinating to him. When Zorn returned to Dalarna in the summer of 1887 he created his first serious work of this kind. It was a study of nude women in combination with pine trees, cliffs, and water. Examination of a number of his photographs (Zorn, like Munch, Degas, and other artists, made systematic use of photography) reveals his deliberate exploration of the interplay between light and shadow, water, and the nude body. During May of the same year, Zorn had visited many exhibitions in Paris, including the Georges Petits Salon where Renoir's *Les Grandes Baigneuses* was on view. It is possible that this painting gave Zorn the impulse to paint nude women in the outdoors.[1]

The manner in which he painted the female body was then relatively new to Swedish art. In contrast to those of his Scandinavian contemporaries, Zorn's nudes are, with few exceptions, without elements of symbolism, allegory, narrative, or literary illusion. In comparison, nudes portrayed by Zorn's contemporaries are depicted in more conventional poses which discreetly confront the viewer in the guise of modesty and/or allegory. Among these are Ernst Josephson's *Watersprite*, 1884, in which the nude is transformed into a folkloric incarnation of wantonness which, at that time, was considered quite lurid.[2] In others, such as Vilhelm Hammershøi's *Female Nude*, 1909–10, the model was posed with head bowed to the side and breasts covered with one arm in a gesture of modesty,[3] while in Eilif Petersen's *Nocturne*, 1887, a languid female with her back to the viewer inhabits an atmospheric landscape.[4]

During the summer of 1888, Zorn conducted his experiments with *valeur* painting, both in oil and in watercolor. *Une première*, a watercolor (see plate 10), received considerable praise and recognition at the Paris Exposition in 1889. Zorn, however, was not happy; he expected more than he was able to achieve in the watercolor medium. The sweeping

41

brush strokes indicate his attempt to push the limitations of the medium beyond its capacity. In his disappointment, Zorn slashed *Une première* to pieces. Later, however, several other versions were executed in oil, watercolor, and etching. Zorn's desire to achieve a more plastic modeling of the play of light over water and the skin of the body made the transition to oil inevitable.[5] The question remains whether Zorn's *valeur* painting ever led to a fully impressionist picture, or, indeed, whether he wanted to achieve pure Impressionism. Regardless, in his rendering, the sensual *rondeur* of the female body was the prevailing essential quality of his nude paintings.

Although Zorn was fascinated by what he perceived to be womanly beauty throughout his career, nudes did not begin to play an important role in his work until the early 1880s. Letters written during his travels would often contain long physical descriptions of the women he had seen. In one, to Claes Adelsköld from Constantinople in 1886, Zorn expressed his amazement that the Greek women he met in the street were as beautiful as their ancestral sisters depicted in ancient sculpture.[6]

Zorn often obtained models by advertising in newspapers, requiring that they have certain physical qualities. Although his models for figure scenes were most often peasant girls from Mora or other parishes in the Siljan Valley, those for the nude paintings were with a few exceptions, professionals.[7] He described his model for *Grotto* as "a primitive type with short strong legs and long arms . . . . The girl was one of those inquisitive, knowledge seeking and fanciful creatures whom one finds among ordinary people in Sweden and who makes collaboration between the artist and his model a delight. This important aspect of an artist's stimulus evoked from the model's side encourages him and makes his work doubly interesting."[8] The model for *Reflections*, a late 1880s work that he considered be extremely difficult to paint, was a sensitive woman who Zorn praised for having grace and patience that, until then, he had only found in his wife, Emma.

Zorn seldom portrayed a particular model, often using several for the same work since, in contrast to his commissioned portraits, it was rarely his objective to render an individual likeness but, rather, to produce a composite that would stand for Woman. He wrote of *Morning Bath*, 1908:

> *What could be more becoming than a girl with a sponge which she squeezes so that the water streams between her fingers. This came upon me quite suddenly. I remembered a water-color I once painted of my wife's back — she stands in a rubber bath and presses a sponge to her breast — I began the same day. The model, or models, were the three sisters Mjoberg whom I has already painted at Gopsmor. What was lacking in one I found in another. I worked on this sculpture with considerable pleasure and I think I succeeded in modeling a really beautiful young female body, so beautiful that in nature I had never seen its equal. This pride and pleasure in his own creation is the most valuable thing an artist*

possesses and he must be allowed to maintain it even if it shows itself to be exaggerated.[9]

Similarly, the sculptor Henry Moore, speaking of his bronze *Seated Woman*, 1957, has said that his own boyhood experience contributed to the conception of its form.

> *I was a Yorkshire miner's son, the youngest of seven, and my mother was no longer so very young. She suffered from bad rheumatism in the back and would often say to me in winter when I came back from school, 'Henry, boy, come and rub my back.' Then I would massage her back with liniment. When I came to this figure which represents a fully mature woman, I found that I was unconsciously giving to its back the long-forgotten shape of the one that I had so often rubbed as a boy.[10]*

Moore, remarking on Cézanne's *Trois Baigneuses*, 1873–77, commented that the reason he liked it so much was because the type of woman Cézanne portrayed was very similar to Moore's romantic ideal of Woman. "Not a young 'slip' of a girl, but a wide, broad, mature woman — matronly, with a strong back not unlike that of a gorilla, with the same kind of flatness."[11]

An analogy can also be seen between Zorn and Manet, whose 1863 works *Olympia* and *Le Déjeuner sur l'Herbe*, had aroused such a storm some thirty years before. Zorn came to admire the work of Manet and there was an affiliation between the two in the person of their mutual friend Antonin Proust and his mistress Rosita Mauri, both of whom Zorn had portrayed in etchings in 1889. Both artists shared a related interest in natural nakedness, in undress, as opposed to the then accepted mythological nudity. Manet's *Olympia*, the prostitute on her bed, is similar to Zorn's Dalecarlian women — not with respect to an ideal of beauty or technique, but in reference to the subject's lack of modesty. However, Manet, by consciously limiting shading, and reducing space to a single dimension, heightened the sense of frankness, combining these elements in a way that compels the viewer to focus on the structure of the picture. Zorn, on the other hand, worked to model the female form so that one could "feel" the back of the body, as one would a sculpture.[12]

Most of Zorn's contemporaries found his nudes to be delightful. Ernest Lang said in 1923: "He presented her as a Brunhilda, naked, unashamed and regal. He reveled in nuances of light playing upon her and her surroundings."[13] French philosopher Henri Focillon wrote: "Zorn is neither classicist or romanticist . . . In an epoch obsessed by intellectualism he stands out by virtue of his frankness and unique candor. Life is beautiful to him, and above all, simple."[14] J. Nilsen Laurvik of *Print Collector's Quarterly* said in 1911:

> *There is in his work something of childlike spontaneity, a healthy, natural enjoyment in the mere practice of his art that is infectious. He has the same impartial love for nature as . . . Velasquez and Franz Hals, and the same interdependence*

of head and hand.[15] With a few swift, sure strokes he gives us the soft contour, the undulating curves of the fresh, firm flesh, of these strong-limbed Junos[16] . . . These big, blond women, whose naked bodies move with unrestrained freedom through the tonic balsam air are imbued with a superb, healthy animalism such as has never been depicted in the whole history of art[17] . . . the exuberant, re-creating force of life is presented in all its tantalizing seductiveness of ample, quivering curves.[18]

Such enthusiasm over Zorn's nudes illustrates how drastically tastes, as well as art criticism, have changed. More recent appraisals are less effusive:

. . . though some of the late bathers such as Three Sisters *displays the artless poses and mindless smiles of a snapshot . . . Though some of the late nudes are simply for "fun," others are serious studies . . . He defused the female nude for a generation of Victorian gentlemen, and possibly for himself as well.[19]*

Mary R. Sullivan

FOOTNOTES

[1]Hans Henrik Brummer, *Zorn Svensk Malare Ivarlden*, (Stockholm: Svalon/Bonniers, 1982), p. 78. As translated by Brigitte Bergman.

[2]Kirk Varnedoe, *Northern Light: Realism and Symbolism in Scandinavian Painting, 1880–1910* (Brooklyn: Brooklyn Museum, 1983), p. 94.

[3]Ibid., p. 136.

[4]Ibid., p. 204.

[5]Brummer, p. 82.

[6]Gerda Boëthius, *Anders Zorn, An International Swedish Artist: His Life and Work* (Stockholm: Nordisk Rotogravyr, 1954), p. 62.

[7]Dan Hofstadter, "Painter-Prince: the return of Anders Zorn," *The New Criterion,* January 1984, p. 30.

[8]Boëthius, p. 67.

[9]Boëthius, pp. 61–62.

[10]Philip James, ed., *Henry Moore On Sculpture* (New York: The Viking Press, 1966), p. 333.

[11]Ibid., p. 208.

[12]Ingela Lind, "Looking Again At Anders Zorn," *Scandinavian Review,* Summer 1984, p. 25.

[13]Ernest M. Lang, *The Etchings of Anders Zorn* (New York: Empire State Book Company, 1923), pp. vi and vii.

[14]Armand Dayot, "The Brilliant Etchings of Anders Zorn," *International Studio,* July 1929, p. 36.

[15]Nilson J. Laurvik, "Anders Zorn — Painter-Etcher," *The Print Collector's Quarterly,* December 1911, pp. 611–622.

[16]Ibid., p. 629.

[17]Ibid., p. 630.

[18]Ibid., p. 635.

[19]Elizabeth Broun, *Prints of Anders Zorn* (Lawrence, Kansas: Spencer Museum of Art, 1979), p. 18.

ANDERS ZORN
THE ACADEMY OF ART

Artists throughout history have traditionally shared many common concerns, among these are: the need for academic training, the struggle to support oneself while developing the necessary artistic skills, and the ability to recognize the point in time when the academic rules can be broken in favor of pursuing one's own style. Anders Leonard Zorn was no exception to these dilemmas. He lived and worked during a period when art and art concepts were undergoing drastic changes.

As a child, Zorn displayed exceptional talent for drawing and wood carving. At the age of fifteen, with encouragement from his mother and the promise of financial backing from his father, Zorn began his artistic training at the Stockholm Academy of Art, an institution firmly rooted in the traditions of practiced copying from antiquity and German genre scenes and of painting monumental pictures of a historical nature. At the academy, Zorn was taught by the reigning masters of contemporary Sweden including the academy's president Johan Christofer Boklund, portrait painter Georg von Rosen, and Carl Wilhelm Palm who was one of the first Swedes known to experiment with etching. Most influential to Zorn was Joseph William Wallander, who painted scenes of Swedish peasant life, particularly from the province of Dalarna in central Sweden, which included Zorn's home town of Mora. All of these men who taught at the academy were quite successful and esteemed during their lifetimes, but their work is now considered to be academic and generally outside the mainstream of Modernism.

Due to economic and geographic factors, Sweden was virtually isolated and cut off from European artistic activity during the nineteenth century. Even so, Swedish museums were slow to recognize the work of their native artists and, typically, large portions of the collections housed in these museums were from the Greek and Roman periods, along with works by Northern European masters. Zorn spent countless hours in the Nationalmuseum studying the works of Rembrandt, one of his earliest influences and one to whom his work would later be compared.

During the last two decades of the nineteenth century, the theory and practice of Impressionism spread throughout the western world. These new ideas from France slowly crept into the academy and created much tension between the masters and the students. Of particular interest among the students was *plein air* painting, the practice of painting out-of-doors. Ambitious Swedish artists interested in learning new methods found it necessary to leave the country to continue their studies. Renowned Swedish sculptor Carl Miles, who also began his education at the academy, left in 1898 to study at École des Beaux-Arts in Paris.

A breakthrough for contemporary Swedish artists came a decade before the Nationalmuseum was to move into its new premises. In a deliberate effort to foster creative art in Sweden, a state subsidy was established for the acquisition of contemporary works. "Masterpieces" were to be chosen that "would be put on exhibition in the Nationalmuseum in that section specially intended for them, as a mark of the highest distinction and reward."[1] The honor of making the selections went to a group of faculty members from the academy, designated as the "Academy of Art."

Opposition grew among the radical artists of the academy. Historical painting, which was very popular at the time, had transformed the museum into a temple of patriotic education, proudly displaying such works as the *Funeral of Charles XII*, and *Eric XIV*. The struggle within the academy reached a peak in 1885 when the young painter, Prince Eugen (son of Queen Sophia and King Oscar II), proposed to present to the museum a major work from the Swedish *plein air* school of painting, *The Watersprite*, by Ernst Josephson. The committee refused to accept it even though Josephson had previously won the Royal Medal for his work, *Sten Sture the Elder Rescuing the Danish Queen Christina from Vadstena Cloister*, a subject often assigned to the students at the academy.

In 1906 the "Society of Swedish Artists" was formed. Founded under the premise that art should be liberated from bureaucratic oppression, it actively opposed the Academy of Art. This opposition led to the division of the Modern Swedish room of the museum so that paintings from the Society of Swedish Artists were hung on the left and those from the Academy of Art hung on the right.

However, it was not until the beginning of World War I that major changes began taking place when Richard Bergh, former academy student and member of the Society of Swedish Artists, was appointed director of the Nationalmuseum. During his five years as director, Bergh, with the help of a state commission dissolved the stern selection committee and arranged for specialists on the museum staff to make decisions regarding acquisitions. He also removed the plaster casts of antique sculptures from the galleries to make room for original Swedish works and, from private donations, began to acquire works from his own generation. In 1946 the museum acquired Josephson's once controversial piece, *The Watersprite*, from the son of Theo van Gogh.

While at the academy, Zorn painted a small oval portrait of Mrs. Hulda Häggström, the daughter of his hostess in Stockholm titled *In Mourning* (figure 2). This, his first work with a veiled subject, was displayed at the academy exhibition in the spring of 1880. Zorn was awarded two hundred crowns for the watercolor, in spite of the fact that he declined to take part in the competitions, refusing to paint prize pictures in favor of more marketable works. The painting sold quickly for 150 crowns (a price set under the advice of Boklund) and received considerable attention. A similar painting titled *The Widow* was painted for King Oscar II, and art critic Carl Rupert Nybolm requested a portrait of his son.

In 1881, after an argument with the academy's new president, Georg von Rosen, Zorn returned his diploma and left the institution. Rosen's complaint was that Zorn's commissions kept him away from class too often. The erratic schedule of payments from his father's estate frequently left him destitute and dependent upon the charity of his father's friends. Zorn had also reached a point where there was little more that formal schooling could offer him, as he was rapidly developing his own style. After leaving the academy, England and Spain were among his first destinations. During his subsequent travels, Zorn was often accompanied by his long time friend Ernst Josephson, who left the academy in 1885 after leading a group of 86 students to resign.

After achieving success in Spain with his watercolors, Zorn sent some samples of his current work to the academy for advice and perhaps some recognition. Even though his departure from the academy was abrupt, he was not one to remain bitter and kept in close contact with many of his former classmates. He was hurt and offended when his work received harsh criticism, but later assumed that it was because they had not yet accepted the impressionistic approach. Although the academicians exerted significant control over Swedish art within both the school and the Nationalmuseum, their strict rules and traditions could not suppress the ambitions or goals of Zorn and his contemporaries, nor could they discourage Zorn's forgiving and generous nature, which is evident in the sizable donation that he sent to the academy shortly before his death.

Karen Sirus

FOOTNOTE

[1]Carl Nordenfalk, *Stockholm* (San Diego: A.S. Barnes and Company, 1969), p. 16.

Plate 9
Modersglädje I (Maternal Delight I), n.d.
Etching
21.4 x 16.3 cm. (8⁷/₈ x 6⁷/₁₆ in.)
Courtesy of Childs Gallery, Boston, Massachusetts

Plate 10
Une première, c. 1888
Watercolor and chalk
33 x 26 cm. (13 x 10¼ in.)
Collection: Sterling and Francine Clark Art Institute, Williamstown, Massachusetts
Not in exhibition

Plate 11
Rosita Mauri, 1889
Etching
31 x 20.9 cm. (13 x 8¼ in.)
Collection: Brigitte Bergman

Plate 12
Zorn and His Wife, 1890
Etching
31.3 x 20.9 cm. (13 x 8¼ in.)
Collection: Spencer Museum of Art, University of Kansas, Lawrence, Gift of the Max Kade Foundation

Plate 13
Cigarettrökerska II (Girl with Cigarette II), 1891
Etching
15.9 x 12 cm. (6¼ x 4¾ in.)
Courtesy of Childs Gallery, Boston, Massachusetts

54

Plate 14
Omnibus, 1892
Etching
27.9 x 19.7 cm. (11 x 7¾ in.)
Courtesy of Childs Gallery, Boston, Massachusetts

55

Plate 15
St. Gaudens with Model, 1897
Etching
13.3 x 19.0 cm. (5¼ x 7½ in.)
Collection: National Portrait Gallery, Smithsonian Institution, Washington, D.C.

Plate 16
Kesti, Paysanne de Mora (Kesti, Mora Peasant Girl), 1906
Etching
15.6 x 12.1 cm. (6⅛ x 4¾ in.)
Collection: Grunwald Center for the Graphic Arts, University of California, Los Angeles

57

Plate 17
Skraṁda (Frightened), 1912
Etching
20 x 15 cm. (7⅞ x 5⅞ in.)
Courtesy of Childs Gallery, Boston, Massachusetts

Plate 18
Syanen (The Swan), 1915
Etching with drypoint
24.8 x 19.7 cm. (9¾ x 7¾ in.)
Courtesy of Childs Gallery, Boston, Massachusetts

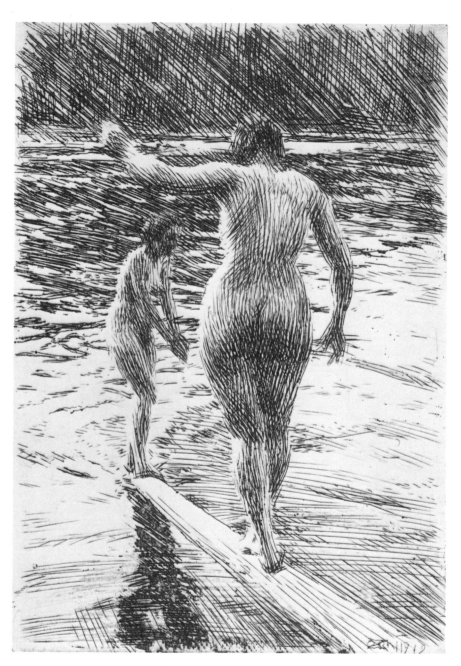

Plate 19
Balance, 1919
Etching
16.7 x 11.2 cm. (6⁵/₈ x 4⁷/₁₆ in.)
Collection: Brigitte Bergman

EXHIBITION LIST

All dimensions are given in centimeters and (inches), height preceding width. Sizes for etchings refer to image size rather than sheet size. An asterisk indicates a plate illustration.

PRINTS AND DRAWINGS

1. *Axel Herman Haig III*, 1884
   Etching
   38.4 x 26 cm. (15¹/₈ x 10¹/₄ in.)
   Collection: Spencer Museum of Art
       University of Kansas, Lawrence
       Gift of the Max Kade Foundation

*2. *Rosita Mauri*, 1889
   Etching
   21.8 x 14.2 cm. (8⁵/₈ x 5⁵/₈ in.)
   Collection: Brigitte Bergman

*3. *Zorn and His Wife*, 1890
   Etching
   31.3 x 20.9 cm. (13 x 8¹/₄ in.)
   Collection: Spencer Museum of Art
       University of Kansas, Lawrence
       Gift of the Max Kade Foundation

*4. *Cigarettrökerska II* (Girl with
       Cigarette II), 1891
   Etching
   15.9 x 12 cm. (6¹/₄ x 4³/₄ in.)
   Courtesy of Childs Gallery
       Boston, Massachusetts

5. *Valsen* (The Waltz), 1891
   Etching
   33.4 x 22.3 cm. (13¹/₄ x 8³/₄ in.)
   Courtesy of Childs Gallery
       Boston, Massachusetts

*6. *Omnibus*, 1892
   Etching
   27.9 x 19.7 cm. (11 x 7³/₄ in.)
   Courtesy of Childs Gallery
       Boston, Massachusetts

7. *Paul Verlaine III*, 1895
   Etching
   24.1 x 16 cm. (9¹/₂ x 6⁵/₁₆ in.)
   Collection: Grunwald Center
       for the Graphic Arts
       University of California
       Los Angeles

8. *Self Portrait with Model*, c. 1897
   Drawing
   27.4 x 21.6 cm. (10¹³/₁₆ x 8¹/₂ in.)
   Collection: National Portrait Gallery
       Smithsonian Institution
       Washington, D.C.

*9. *St. Gaudens and Model*, 1897
   Etching
   13.3 x 19 cm. (5¹/₄ x 7¹/₂ in.)
   Collection: National Portrait Gallery
       Smithsonian Institution
       Washington, D.C.

10. *Maud Cassel (Mrs. Ashley)*, 1898
    Etching
    17.9 x 12.8 cm. (7 x 5 in.)
    Collection: Spencer Museum of Art
        University of Kansas, Lawrence
        Gift of the Max Kade Foundation

*11. *Self Portrait with Model II*, 1899
    Etching
    24.5 x 17.6 cm. (9⅝ x 7 in.)
    Collection: Spencer Museum of Art
        University of Kansas, Lawrence
        Gift of the Max Kade Foundation

12. *Joueuse de guitare* (The Guitar
    Player), 1900
    Etching
    23.8 x 16 cm. (9⅜ x 6⅝ in.)
    Collection: Brigitte Bergman

13. *Emma Rassmussen*, 1904
    Etching
    19.5 x 14.9 cm. (7⅞ x 5⅞ in.)
    Collection: Spencer Museum of Art
        University of Kansas, Lawrence
        Gift of the Max Kade Foundation

14. *Byspelman* (The Village Violinist), 1904
    Etching
    16.1 x 12 cm. (6⅝ x 4¾ in.)
    Collection: Brigitte Bergman

15. *Betty Nansen*, 1905
    Etching
    25 x 17.4 cm. (9⅞ x 6⅞ in.)
    Collection: Grunwald Center
        for the Graphic Arts
        University of California
        Los Angeles

16. *Anatole France*, 1906
    Etching
    21.3 x 16.1 cm. (8⅜ x 6⅜ in.)
    Collection: The Art Institute of Chicago

*17. *Kesti, Paysanne de Mora* (Kesti, Mora
    Peasant Girl), 1906
    Etching
    15.6 x 12.1 cm. (6⅛ x 4¾ in.)
    Collection: Grunwald Center
        for the Graphic Arts
        University of California
        Los Angeles

18. *Raccommodage* (Mending), 1906
    Etching
    20 x 14.8 cm. (7⅞ x 5¹³⁄₁₆ in.)
    Collection: Grunwald Center
        for the Graphic Arts
        University of California
        Los Angeles

19. *M. and Mme. Atherton Curtis*, 1906
    Etching
    24.3 x 18.4 cm. (9⅜ x 7¼ in.)
    Collection: Grunwald Center
        for the Graphic Arts
        University of California
        Los Angeles

20. *Prince Paul Troubetskoy II*, 1909
    Etching
    24.5 x 17.4 cm. (9⅝ x 6⅞ in.)
    Collection: Mills College Art Gallery,
        Oakland, California

21. *August Strindberg,* 1910
    Etching
    29.5 x 19.7 cm. (11⁵/₈ x 7³/₄ in.)
    Collection: The Art Institute of Chicago

*22. *Skrämda* (Frightened), 1912
    Etching
    20 x 15 cm. (7⁷/₈ x 5⁷/₈ in.)
    Courtesy of Childs Gallery
        Boston, Massachusetts

23. *Hårbandet* (The Hair Ribbon), 1912
    Etching
    34.3 x 25.3 (13¹/₂ x 9³/₄ in.)
    Collection: Los Angeles County
        Museum of Art
        Gift of Wallace L. DeWolf

24. *Professor John Berg,* 1912
    Etching
    16.7 x 11.2 cm. (6⁹/₁₆ x 4⁷/₁₆ in.)
    Collection: Brigitte Bergman

25. *Vallkulla,* 1912
    Etching
    30 x 19.7 cm. (11⁷/₈ x 7⁷/₈ in.)
    Collection: Spencer Museum of Art
        University of Kansas, Lawrence
        Gift of the Max Kade Foundation

*26. *Syanen* (The Swan), 1915
    Etching with drypoint
    24.8 x 19.7 cm. (9³/₄ x 17³/₄ in.)
    Courtesy of Childs Gallery
        Boston, Massachusetts

27. *Mes modèles* (My Models) 1916
    Etching
    20.3 x 14.8 cm. (7¹³/₁₆ x 5¹³/₁₆ in.)
    Collection: Grunwald Center
        for the Graphic Arts
        University of California
        Los Angeles

28. *Självporträtt* (Self Portrait), 1916
    Etching with drypoint
    29 x 20 cm. (11⁷/₁₆ x 8 in.)
    Collection: Wadsworth Atheneum
        Hartford, Connecticut, Bequest of
        George A. Gay

29. *Gulli II,* 1918
    Etching
    19.7 x 14.6 cm. (7³/₄ x 5³/₄ in.)
    Collection: Mills College Art Gallery
        Oakland, California

*30. *Balance,* 1919
    Etching
    16.7 x 11.2 cm. (6⁵/₈ x 4⁷/₁₆ in.)
    Collection: Brigitte Bergman

31. *Ols Maria,* 1919
    Etching
    19.2 x 28.8 cm. (7⁹/₁₆ x 11³/₈ in.)
    Collection: Mills College Art Gallery
        Oakland, California

32. *La Baigneuse* (The Bather), 1919
    Etching
    17.8 x 12.1 cm. (7 x 4¹¹/₁₆ in.)
    Collection: Grunwald Center
        for the Graphic Arts
        University of California
        Los Angeles

*33. *Modersglädje I* (Maternal Delight I), n.d.
Etching
21.3 x 16.2 cm. (8³⁄₈ x 6³⁄₈ in.)
Courtesy of Childs Gallery
Boston, Massachusetts

*34. *Mrs. Charles Deering*, n.d.
Monotype
31.5 x 23.5 cm. (12³⁄₈ x 9¹⁄₄ in.)
Collection: The Art Institute of Chicago

35. *St. Gaudens and Model*, n.d.
Drawing
21.9 x 27.9 cm. (8⁵⁄₈ x 11 in.)
Courtesy of Childs Gallery
Boston, Massachusetts

PAINTINGS

36. *Fjärilarna* (Butterflies), 1884–85
Watercolor
25.4 x 35.4 cm. (10 x 13¹⁵⁄₁₆ in.)
Collection: Zornmuseet, Mora, Sweden

37. *Landskap med aloe* (Landscape
with Aloe), 1887
Watercolor
25.5 x 18 cm. (10¹⁄₁₆ x 7¹⁄₈ in.)
Collection: Zornmuseet, Mora, Sweden

38. *Mustapha Reis, North Africa*, 1887
Watercolor
20.9 x 27.2 cm. (8¹⁄₈ x 10³⁄₄ in.)
Collection: Zornmuseet, Mora, Sweden

39. *Sierra Nevada, Spain*, 1887
Watercolor
25.4 x 35.4 cm. (10 x 13¹⁵⁄₁₆ in.)
Collection: Zornmuseet, Mora, Sweden

40. *Sjö studien* (Sea Study), 1887
Watercolor
20.9 x 27 cm. (8¹⁄₈ x 10⁵⁄₈ in.)
Collection: Zornmuseet, Mora, Sweden

*41. Untitled (Scandinavian Maid?), 1889
Oil on board
35.6 x 35.6 cm. (14 x 14 in.)
Courtesy of de ville galleries, inc.
Los Angeles

42. *Atlanten* (The Atlantic Ocean)
c. 1890–96
Watercolor
12.6 x 10 cm. (5 x 3¹⁵⁄₁₆ in.)
Collection: Zornmuseet, Mora, Sweden

43. *Beach in Folkestone, England*, 1890
Watercolor
14 x 23.5 cm. (5$\frac{1}{2}$ x 9$\frac{1}{4}$ in.)
Collection: Zornmuseet, Mora, Sweden

44. *Från Nordkap* (From the North
Cape), 1890
Watercolor
31.6 x 22.6 cm. (12$\frac{5}{8}$ x 8$\frac{7}{8}$ in.)
Collection: Zornmuseet, Mora, Sweden

45. *Trondhjen, Norway I*, 1890
Watercolor
11.9 x 17 cm. (4$\frac{11}{16}$ x 6$\frac{11}{16}$ in.)
Collection: Zornmuseet, Mora, Sweden

46. *Trondhjen, Norway II*, 1890
Watercolor
11.9 x 17 cm. (4$\frac{11}{16}$ x 6$\frac{11}{16}$ in.)
Collection: Zornmuseet, Mora, Sweden

47. *Atlanten* (The Atlantic Ocean), 1894
Watercolor
12.6 x 19.6 cm. (5 x 7$\frac{15}{16}$ in.)
Collection: Zornmuseet, Mora, Sweden

48. *Vågsvallen* (The Surf), 1894
Watercolor
12.6 x 20 cm. (4$\frac{7}{8}$ x 7$\frac{7}{8}$ in.)
Collection: Zornmuseet, Mora, Sweden

49. *Venice, Italy*, 1894
Watercolor
38 x 28 cm. (14$\frac{15}{16}$ x 11$\frac{1}{16}$ in.)
Collection: Zornmuseet, Mora, Sweden

*50. *William Taussig*, 1897
Oil on canvas
81.3 x 66 cm. (32 x 26 in.)
Collection: The J.B. Speed Art
    Museum, Louisville, Kentucky
    Gift of Miss Adele Brandeis

*51. *Frances Folsom Cleveland*
    (Mrs. Grover), 1899
Oil on canvas
137.2 x 92.1 cm. (54 x 36$\frac{1}{4}$ in.)
Collection: National Portrait Gallery
    Smithsonian Institution
    Washington, D.C.
    Gift of Mrs. Frances Payne

*52. *Mrs. Dan Cameron*, 1900
Oil on canvas
147.3 x 113.3 cm. (58 x 44$\frac{1}{2}$ in.)
Collection: National Museum of
    American Art, Smithsonian
    Institution, Washington, D.C.
    Gift of Anonymous Donor

53. *Samuel Untermeyer*, 1901
Oil on canvas
120.2 x 76.8 cm. (40$\frac{1}{4}$ x 30$\frac{1}{4}$ in.)
Collection: The New York Historical
    Society, New York

*54. *Flickan från Elfdalen* (The Girl from
    Elfdalen), n.d.
Oil on canvas
90.1 x 61 cm. (35$\frac{1}{2}$ x 24 in.)
Collection: The Minneapolis Institute of
    Arts, Lillian Z. Turnblad Fund

Photo: Custom Graphics, from *Anders Zorn: Själbiografiska anteckningar* (Stockholm: Albert Bonniers Förlag AB, 1982.)

Anders and Emma Zorn, 1920
Photograph

LENDERS TO THE EXHIBITION

The Art Institute of Chicago
Brigitte Bergman
Childs Gallery, New York and Boston
de ville galleries, inc., Los Angeles
Grunwald Center for the Graphic Arts, University of California, Los Angeles
The J.B. Speed Art Museum, Louisville, Kentucky
Los Angeles County Museum of Art
Mills College Art Gallery, Oakland, California
The Minneapolis Institute of the Arts
National Museum of American Art, Smithsonian Institution, Washington, D.C.
National Portrait Gallery, Smithsonian Institution, Washington, D.C.
The New York Historical Society, New York
Spencer Museum of Art, University of Kansas, Lawrence
Wadsworth Atheneum, Hartford, Connecticut
Zornmuseet, Mora, Sweden

BIBLIOGRAPHY

Adeline, Jules. *The Adeline Art Dictionary*. New York: Frederick Ungar Publishing Company, 1966.

Allhusen, E.L. "Anders Zorn: Some Personal Recollections." *International Studio*, November 1920, pp. 94–96.

American Art News October 16, 1920, pp. 5–6.

"Anders Zorn: The Swedish Maupassant in Art." *The American Review of Reviews*, May 1910, pp. 613–614.

Art Journal, Winter 1979, pp. 141.

"The Art of Anders Zorn." *The New York Times*, August 29, 1920

Asplund, Karl. *Anders Zorn, His Life and His Work*. Edited by Geoffrey Holm. Translated by Henry Alexander. London: The Studio. Chicago: A. Kroch and Company, 1921.

Boëthius, Gerda. *Anders Zorn, An International Swedish Artist: His Life and Work*. Stockholm: Nordisk Rotogravyr, 1954.

_____ . *Zorn, Swedish Painter and World Traveller*. Stockholm: Raben and Sjogren, 1959; reprint ed., 1961.

Blauvelt, Hiram Bellis. "Zorn's Fingertips." *American Magazine of Art*, February 1925, pp. 87–90.

Broun, Elizabeth. *Prints of Anders Zorn*. Lawrence, Kansas: Spencer Museum of Art, University of Kansas, 1979.

Browne, Rosaline. "Anders Zorn: Exhibition at A.A.A. Gallery." *ARTnews*, October 1967, p. 67.

_____ . *Zorn Engravings (A Complete Catalogue)*. Uppsala, Sweden: Hjert & Hjert, 1980.

Brummer, Dr. Hans Henrik. *Zorn Svensk Malare Ivarlden*. Portions translated by Brigitte Bergman. Stockholm: Svalon/Bonniers, Förlag AB, 1975.

_____ . *Anders Zorn: Självbiografiska anteckningar*. Stockholm: Albert Bonniers Förlag AB, 1982.

Brunius, Teddy and Reutersvärd, Oscar. *Samtal om Zorn*. Czechoslovakia: Bokförlaget Trevi, 1979.

Caffin, Charles. "Zorn's Gift as Etcher Exhibited." *New York American*, October 6, 1913.

Dayot, Armand. "The Brilliant Etchings of Anders Zorn." *International Studio*, July 1929, pp. 32–36.

Frantz, Henri. "A Note on the Recent Work of Anders Zorn." *International Studio*, October 1906, pp. 281–289.

Gerdts, William H. *American Impressionism*. Seattle: The Henry Art Gallery, University of Washington, 1980.

Hamilton, George Heard. *19th and 20th Century Art*. New York: Harry N. Abrams, Inc., 1970.

Hannover, Emil.; Lauren, Carl.; and Thiis, Jens. *Scandinavian Art*. London: Humphrey Milford Oxford University Press, 1922.

Hofstadter, Dan. "Painter Prince: the return of Anders Zorn." *The New Criterion*, January 1984, pp. 26-36.

James, Philip, ed. *Henry Moore on Sculpture*. New York: The Viking Press, 1966.

Lang, Ernest M. *The Etchings of Anders Zorn*. New York: Empire State Book Company, 1923.

Laurin, Carl G. "A Swedish Painter and Etcher: Anders Zorn." *International Studio*, 1898, pp. 164–170.

Laurvik, J. Nilson. "Anders Zorn — Painter-Etcher." *The Print Collector's Quarterly*, December 1911, pp. 610–637.

Lind, Ingela. "Looking Again at Anders Zorn." *Scandinavian* Review, Summer 1984.

Norderflak, Carl. *Stockholm*. San Diego: A.S. Barnes and Company, 1969.

(Obituary). *The New York Times*, October 23, 1921.

"The Power of Anders Zorn." *The New York Times*, August 24, 1920.

"Recalling a Quarrel: Portrait of Henry Clay Pierce, by Anders Zorn." *Art Digest*, January 1, 1934, p. 17.

Saarinen, Aline Bernstein. *The Proud Possessors*. London: Weidenfield and Nicholson, 1958.

Sadik, Marvin. "Paintings from the White House." *Connoisseur*, May 1976, p. 22.

Sweet, Frederick A. "Great Chicago Collectors." *Apollo*, September 1966, pp. 203–206.

Tharp, Louise. *Mrs. Jack*. Boston: Little, Brown and Company, 1965.

Van Rensselaer, M.G. "A Swedish Etcher." *Century Magazine*. August 1893, pp. 582–589.

Varnedoe, Kirk. *Northern Light: Realism and Symbolism in Scandinavian Painting*, 1880–1910. Brooklyn: The Brooklyn Museum, 1982.

Weimann, Jeanne Madeline. *The Fair Women*. Chicago: Academy of Chicago, 1981.

"Zorn: King's Artist is Dead in Sweden." *The New York Times*, August 23, 1920.

"Zorn in Kansas — Travelling Exhibition." *Apollo*, October 1980, p. 279.

PHOTO CREDITS

The Art Institute of Chicago: plate no. 8 and figure 3; Childs Gallery: plate nos. 9, 13, 14, 17, 18; Clark Art Institute: plate no. 10; Custom Graphics: plate nos. 11, 19 and figures 1, 2, 4, 5, 6; de ville galleries: plate no. 1; Isabella Stewart Gardner Museum: plate no. 2; Grunwald Center for the Graphic Arts: plate no. 16; The J.B. Speed Art Museum: plate no. 3; The Minneapolis Institute of Arts: plate no. 7; Nationalmuseum, Stockholm: plate no. 5; National Museum of American Art: plate no. 6; National Portrait Gallery: plate nos. 4, 15; Spencer Museum of Art: plate no. 12.

COLOPHON

This catalogue was designed in Newport Beach, California by Kirsten Jacobs Whalen
Type was set in Goudy Roman by Queen Beach Printers, Inc., Long Beach, California
Lithographed in an edition of 1,500 on 100# Sonata Kidskin by Queen Beach Printers, Inc.